Dedications

Compiled by Iran Sanadzadeh

For Alberto and Octavio, whom I call
by other names

For Jonny Brock and Clare Gorst
And all other Arlingtonians for
Tea, sympathy and a sofa

For Pilar
For my daughter
Violante
for jomi garcia ascot
and maria luisa elio

For
FELIX and HEDI
In Long and Affectionate Friendship

Dedicated to my wife, without whom this book would not have been written; and to my parents, whose faith started it all.

For Marie d'Estournelles de Constant

À M. Gaston Calmette.
Comme un témiognage de profonde
et affectueuse reconnaissance.
M. P.

For my parents
And
Jonathan

For Paul

TO THE HALLOWED
MEMORY OF
GUSTAV MAHLER

A Charles Levadé

To Kate

TO MY GRANDMOTHER

To Whom It May Concern

For Peter M.,
With gratitude

for Pop, who sees the stars and Jude, who hears their music

This book is for Ken Corbett

In memory of Michel Waisvisz (1949-2008),
who showed us how to touch electronics.

To Marisa

To Liana

In memory

of my mother and my older sister, Mina,

both of whom passed away

during the writing of this book.

TO JIM SHARMAN

To Martin

Ives wrote and dedicated the *Memos*
to answer questions
from people curious about his music.
In his mind and heart
it was dedicated to them all.

This Child is Augusta's

Let us with tuneful skill proclaim these
generations of the Gods,
That one may see them when these hymns are chanted in a future
age.

(Rgveda 10.72.1)

"It was clear to me for a long time that
the origins of science had their deep roots
in a particular myth, that of *invariance*."
(Giorgio de Santillana, Preface to *HAMLET'S MILL*)

To the memory of my son
Kāmrān

To my father, Donald E. Clarke,
who taught me, not with words but by his
example, to do the best I could;
to Joe and Sol Hoffman, for much
the same reason;
and in memory of Joseph Hollingsworth Igo
and Elmer Hugo Reuss -
all Wisconsin men, good and true

*To Moloojoon, Baba Akbar, Maryam,
Paola, and Marianna*

To my husband
Frank Elmer Wood

To the students in the school
from which we'll never graduate

To my beloved family
and in memory of Sidney Cowell, who did not
live to read it

Dedicated to:
Frankie Lymon
Ahmad Jamal
Paul Desmond
Werne Marsh
Dinah Washington
John Coltrane
Ornette Coleman
Arnold Schönberg
Lil Hardin-Armstrong
Karlheinz Stockhausen
John Cage
Hildegard von Bingen
Muhal Bichard Abrams

Dedicated to the memory of
Takemoto Tosahiro
(1897-1992)

For Sherry and Renée
To the memory of my parents and godson

TO H. G. WELLS
The chronicler of Mr Leisham's love
the biographer of Kipps and the
historian of the ages to come
this simple tale of the nineteenth century
is affectionately offered

*To my co-workers on
the World Soundscape Project*

Sources
In order of appearance

Lahiri, Jhumpa. 2004. *The Namesake*. Boston, New York: Mariner Books.
Adams, Douglas. 1984. *The Hitchhiker's Guide to the Galaxy*. London: Pan Macmillan.
Saramago, Jose. 1997. *Blindness*. Orlando: Harvest, Harcourt Brace and Company.
Márquez, Gabriel García. 1967/2009. Camberwell: Penguin.
Carner, Mosco. 1975. *Alban Berg: The Man and the Work*. London: Duckworth.
Cope, David. 1971. *New Directions in Music*. Iowa: WM. C. Brown Publishers.
White, Patrick. 1957, *Voss*. New York: Viking Press.
Proust, Marcel. 1922/2005. *In Search of Lost Time, Volume 1: Swann's way*. London: Vintage.
Ross, Alex. 2007. *The Rest is Noise*. New York: Farrar, Straus and Giroux.
Wan, James. 2015. *Furious 7*. New York: Universal Pictures.
Schonberg, Arnold. 1911/1978. *Theory of Harmony*. Berkeley and Los Angeles: University of California Press.
Satie, Erik. 1888. *3me Gymnopédie*.
Farnell, Andy. 2010. *Designing Sound*. Cmabridge, MA: MIT Press.
Collins, Karen. 2008. *Game Sound*. Cambridge, MA: MIT Press.
Cage, John. 1973. *Silence*. Middletown, CT: Wesleyan.
Egan, Jennifer. 2011. *A Visit from the Good Squad*. London: Hachette.
Catton, Eleanor. 2013. *The Luminaries*. London: Granta.
Cunningham, Michael. 1998/2003. *The Hours*. Netley, SA: Griffin.
Collins, Nicolas. 2006. *Handmade Electronic Music*. New York: Routledge.
Margis, Claudio. 1997/1999. *Microcosms*. London: The Harvill Press.
Burgess, Anthony. 1980. *Earthly Powers*. Croydon: Vintage.
Ebadi, Shirin. 2006. *Iran Awakening*. New York: Random House.
White, Patrick. 1979. *The Twyborn Affair*. London: Penguin.
McVay, Gordon. 1994. *Chekhov: A Life in Letters*. London: The Folio Society.
Kirkpatrick, John (ed.)1972. *Ives, Charle E. Memos*. New York: W. W. Norton and Company, Inc.
McClain, Ernest G. 1984. *The Myth of Invariance*. New York: Nicolas Hays Ltd.
Farhat, Hormoz. 1990. *The Dastgāh Concept in Persian Music*.Cambridge: Cambridge University Press.
Clarke, Donald (ed.) 1998. *The Penguin Encyclopedia of Popular Music*. Ann Arbor, MI: The University of Michigan Press.
Bahari, Maziar and Aimee Molloy. 2011. *Then They Came for Me: A Family's Story of Love, captivity and Survival*. NewYork: Random House.

Wood, Mary Cokely. 1951. *Flower Arrangement Art of Japan.* Tokyo: Dai Nippon Printing.

Cage, John. 1973. *Empty Words.* Middletown, CT: Wesleyan University Press.

Sachs, John. 202. *Henry Cowell: A Man Made of Music.* New York: Oxford University Press.

Braxton, Anthony. 1988. *Composition Notes Book A.* N/A: Synthesis Music.

Coaldrake, A. Kimi. 1997. *Women's Gidayū* and the Japanese Theatre Tradition. London: Routledge.

Naussbaum, Charles O. 2007. *The Musical Representation: Meaning, Ontology and Emotion.* Cambridge, MA: MIT Press.

Conrad, Joseph. 1907/1963. *The Secret Agent.* Middlesex: Penguin.

Schafer, R. Murray. 1977. *The Soundscape: Our Sonic Environment and the Tuning of the World.* Rochester, Vermont: Destiny Books.